AF270623

Cyclopes

by Grace Hansen

abdobooks.com

Published by Abdo Kids, a division of ABDO, P.O. Box 398166, Minneapolis, Minnesota 55439.
Copyright © 2024 by Abdo Consulting Group, Inc. International copyrights reserved in all countries.
No part of this book may be reproduced in any form without written permission from the publisher.
Abdo Kids Jumbo™ is a trademark and logo of Abdo Kids.

Printed in the United States of America, North Mankato, Minnesota.

102023

012024

THIS BOOK CONTAINS
RECYCLED MATERIALS

Photo Credits: Alamy, Everette Collection, Getty Images, Shutterstock,
©ScottKazama p22 / CC BY-SA, ©Oganesson p22 / CC BY-SA

Production Contributors: Teddy Borth, Jennie Forsberg, Grace Hansen
Design Contributors: Candice Keimig, Pakou Moua

Library of Congress Control Number: 2023937671
Publisher's Cataloging-in-Publication Data

Names: Hansen, Grace, author.

Title: Cyclopes / by Grace Hansen

Description: Minneapolis, Minnesota : Abdo Kids, 2024 | Series: World of mythical beings | Includes online
    resources and index.

Identifiers: ISBN 9781098268565 (lib. bdg.) | ISBN 9781098269265 (ebook) | ISBN 9781098269616
    (Read-to-Me ebook)

Subjects: LCSH: Cyclopes (Greek mythology)-- Juvenile literature. | Mythical animals--Juvenile literature. |
    Folklore--Juvenile literature. | Legends--Juvenile literature.

Classification: DDC 398.2454--dc23

Table of Contents

Myth of the Cyclops 4

Two Kinds 6

Cyclopes Today 18

Modern Cyclopes
Based in Mythology 22

Glossary 23

Index 24

Abdo Kids Code 24

Myth of the Cyclops

Cyclopes are giant one-eyed creatures who first appeared in Greek mythology.

Two Kinds

There were two main types of cyclopes in Greek mythology. These two types were described by Hesiod and Homer. Hesiod and Homer were Greek poets who lived in the 700s BCE.

Homer
Hesiod

Hesiod's three cyclopes were powerful giants. They were the sons of Uranus (sky) and Gaia (Earth). The three brothers **forged** weapons for the gods.

Cronus, a Titan, was afraid of cyclopes. He imprisoned them in the **underworld**. He feared his children too and ate most of them, except Zeus. Zeus would later free the cyclopes.

The cyclopes **forged** weapons
for war against the Titans.
They made Zeus a thunderbolt,
Poseidon a trident, and Hades
a helmet. With these, the gods
beat the Titans.

War of the
Titans

Homer's cyclopes were described
in the **Odyssey**. These one-eyed
giants lived on an island. They
were **violent**, not very smart, and
ate humans.

Homer's famous cyclops is
named Polyphemus. He is the
son of Poseidon. The hero
Odysseus blinded Polyphemus.

Cyclopes Today

Cyclopes are still popular creatures today. They are featured in literature, television, and movies. Mike Wazowski of *Monsters Inc.* is a lovable cyclops!

The cyclops played an important role in Greek mythology. The one-eyed giant continues to capture the imaginations of people around the world.

Modern Cyclopes Based in Mythology

Cyclops
Marvel Superhero

- Leader of the X-Men
- Has the ability to shoot powerful beams of energy from his eyes
- His eyewear gives the appearance of having only one eye

Stuart (minion)
Despicable Me Franchise

- Works for the supervillain Gru
- Good at building things, such as spaceships and toys
- Always hungry

Turanga Leela
Futurama

- Born in the year 2975
- Captain and pilot on board the *Planet Express Ship*
- Skilled martial artist

Glossary

forged – to form or shape by heating and hammering.

Odyssey – an epic poem by the ancient Greek poet Homer recounting the adventures of Odysseus on his long voyage home from the Trojan Wars.

underworld – in Greek mythology, a distinct realm where an individual goes after death.

violent – acting with great force or ill will.

Index

appearance 4, 8, 14

characteristics 8, 14

Cronus 10

Greek mythology 6, 8, 10, 12, 14, 16, 20

Hades 12

Hesiod 6, 8, 10, 12

Homer 6, 14, 16

Mike Wazowski 18

Monsters Inc. 18

Odysseus 16

Odyssey 14

Polyphemus 16

Poseidon 12, 16

Titans 10, 12

weapons 8, 12

Zeus 10, 12

Abdo Kids
ONLINE
FREE! ONLINE MULTIMEDIA RESOURCES

Visit **abdokids.com** to access crafts, games, videos, and more!

Use Abdo Kids code **WCK8565** or scan this QR code!